THE STATIONS OF THE CROSS

THE STATIONS OF THE CROSS

Fr Bryan Shortall OFM Cap

VERITAS

Published 2023 by
Veritas Publications
7–8 Lower Abbey Street
Dublin 1
Ireland
publications@veritas.ie
www.veritas.ie

ISBN 978 1 80097 055 7

With ecclesiastical approval, ✠ Dermot Farrell, Archbishop of Dublin

10 9 8 7 6 5 4 3 2 1

Designed and typeset by Padraig McCormack, Veritas Publications
Printed in the Republic of Ireland by Walsh Colour Print, Kerry

Veritas Publications is a member of Publishing Ireland.

Veritas books are printed on paper made from the wood pulp of managed forests. For every tree felled, at least one tree is planted, thereby renewing natural resources.

CONTENTS

PREFACE

A few years ago, I remember having a conversation with an artist who was approached by a priest and asked would he consider painting a set of the Stations of the Cross for the church. I recall thinking that this would take some time to do.

When I was a postulant in the Capuchin Franciscan Order (1987–88), we lived in the Capuchin Friary in Carlow and we had a lovely set of the Stations of the Cross painted by a Poor Clare nun, Sr John Francis (now gone to her reward), from across the River Barrow in their monastery in Graiguecullen. They were beautiful with rich colours, and they really invited the person to walk the Way of the Cross with Christ. When the friary closed recently the stations returned to the Poor Clare Monastery in Graiguecullen. I am always thankful to the Poor Clare nuns as they are a powerhouse of prayer for all who are in need. In this day and age their prayerful support is vital for our world.

My idea for the Stations of the Cross was as an aid to meditation and prayer, whereby drawing and colouring, I would get a powerful sense of the suffering Christ and try to build a bridge to pray for all who asked for my prayers and for all who suffer.

The drawings were made around 2015–16, and I wrote the reflections during the Covid-19 pandemic as an aid to make the Stations of the Cross with our 'rosary family' on social media during the lockdowns. A little time has passed since then and we are continuing to hear about Covid-19 across the world and are being urged to take care. Now, we are in the midst of a war in Europe and Ukraine and its people have been suffering enormously. We pray for an end to the conflict and a new beginning of diplomacy and peace. There are other places where warfare and violence are crushing the people, especially the innocent, and societies and peoples are walking the Way of the Cross daily.

We pray for this Good Friday experience to give way to an Easter Sunday of new hope and new life.

November 2022

ACKNOWLEDGEMENTS

I am grateful to Br Sean Kelly, provincial minister, for his fraternal support from day one.

I appreciate the support of Archbishop Dermot Farrell in the final preparations of the book.

To the parishioners of St Francis of Assisi Parish, Priorswood, for their love and kindness. Despite the challenges, we journeyed and prayed together (at a social distance) during pandemic years 2019–22.

I am thankful to Fr Cory Muresan, Aughrim Street Parish and Romanian Greek-Catholic chaplain, for his advice and support.

I thank Paddy Pender for her advice on the arrangements of the artwork and reflections.

I appreciate the support of Natalie Meleady in the parish office in Priorswood who assisted in putting together this book.

To Brs Terence Harrington and Bill Ryan for their fraternal kindness.

Finally, I am grateful to Síne Quinn, Angela Olejnik, Padraig McCormack, Lir MacCárthaigh, David Macken and all the team at Veritas for all the support in the publication of this book.

I dedicate this book to our Priorswood rosary family, who from the beginning of the restrictions and the lockdowns joined us nightly to pray the rosary, not just from the parish and from Ireland, but across the world.

Nil Desperandum

Fr Bryan Shortall OFM Cap
November 2022

INTRODUCTION

The Stations of the Cross have been part of many people's lives over the years. I have some childhood memories of attending the Stations of the Cross in the different Dublin parishes we lived in growing up. In the quiet and solemnity of Good Friday, the Stations of the Cross at noon was always very well attended and still is to this day.

As novices in our Capuchin Friary in Kilkenny, part of the 'horarium' or timetable every Friday was to make the Stations of the Cross. I used to make them after supper on a Friday evening after the church closed. When I was a student friar, I was edified by one of our church sacristans in Dublin who would faithfully make the Stations of the Cross every day on his arrival into the church. He would genuflect on beginning each station and spend a little time at each one. When he got to the twelfth, the crucifixion, he would kneel in prayer for a few moments before continuing. This example has stayed with me, and I am once again reminded how the journey of Christ to Calvary can help all who struggle and suffer in life, and how we can pray for others.

I illustrated a set of the Stations of the Cross over a couple of months at the end of 2015 and early 2016. I lit a candle and tried to pray the rosary as I drew. I found from my memories of the stations, the scriptures and well-known pictures of the suffering Jesus, that I was able to convey the passion Jesus endured.

In each picture I drew the Holy Spirit as a dove. I wanted to show the Holy Spirit as the Sanctifier who empowers us to cope with hardships and suffering. The Holy Spirit comes upon us at our baptism and at confirmation bestowing the seven gifts: wisdom, understanding, strength, counsel, knowledge, piety and wonder and awe in God's presence. I have used these drawings in my own meditations over the years. I have also used them during the pandemic, during Lent 2020 and again in 2021, which coincided with Level 5 restrictions in Ireland.

We have endured a once-in-a-century pandemic since the last weeks of 2019 and into early 2020. At the time of writing, spring 2022, Covid-19 is still in the community and we are encouraged to be careful, although there are hopeful signs all around us. This highly transmissible virus has made people extremely sick, and many people have died across the world. Many are living with 'long Covid' symptoms, which leave people weak and debilitated for months afterwards.

Thankfully, good science and medical advice has helped us to be as safe as possible, but for the best part of two years we all endured restrictions in how we interacted with each other. Gatherings were forbidden, and there were lockdowns where people were very restricted as to where they went in their neighbourhoods. Schools were closed and religious services were confined to online streaming and social media.

Meetings and business were primarily conducted via various media such as Zoom and families were unable to meet and gather. Face masks became part of the uniform and while the surgical and medical kind were recommended, bespoke masks were worn by many. Our elderly citizens were asked to 'cocoon' indoors away from any risk of meeting people where the virus could spread and compromise health. We all saw pictures of grandparents inside living room windows while the grandchildren were gathered outside in the garden. Elderly parents waving to adult children from behind the nursing home glass. It was awful. We have lost two years of our lives to this pandemic but of course many people lost so much more.

This was our 'Way of the Cross'. The Covid-19 pandemic has brought immense suffering to the world and while countries were dealing with their own national response to it, the challenges varied in different places. Day and night, social media and the mass media reported the latest stories of Covid-19 across the world. For a while it was hard to hear all the shocking news, but it was compelling, nonetheless. We craved

good news and hopeful stories, and they came and went. There was certainly an element of solidarity, in that humanity was all in it together.

Thanks to talented virologists, scientists, innovative research, and a political and social will, vaccines came into being, reducing the worst effects of the virus and preventing serious illness, hospitalisation, and death.

We give thanks for all who kept vigil and provided frontline services during the pandemic: nurses, doctors, medical staff, care staff, general practices, emergency services, parishes, chaplaincies, pastoral carers, and all frontline staff who were out helping others when we had to stay in; the airline pilots and airport staff who made it possible for hospitals to receive PPE; those who developed and administered our vaccines. They were the ones who helped us carry the cross and made the going a bit easier. God bless their healing hands. We were never more together although we had to be physically apart.

April 2022

THE FIRST STATION

Jesus is Condemned to Death

We adore you, O Christ, and we bless you,
Because by your holy cross you have redeemed the world.

There is huge drama in the encounter between Pilate and Jesus. The established church leadership at the time knew they had no power to crucify anyone. The religious leaders had to seek the authority of the political. Pilate was Caesar's man in that region and therefore he had the power to sentence a man to death as a criminal.

As the drama unfolded, Pilate was not certain of the guilt of Jesus. Though the established church leadership at the time tried to convince him that Jesus was a menace to society, Jesus was no criminal or danger to the peace. While Jesus stepped on a few toes and challenged the Pharisees and the Scribes, he was hardly going to succeed in bringing about an end to Rome.

Pilate was put under pressure to do away with Jesus so he had him scourged in a bid to see if that would placate the rabble. Jesus was brought back in an awful state, almost whipped to within an inch of his life. There is much to learn about walking the Way of the Cross with Jesus. On the face of it, Roman punishments are bloody and grotesque. The deeper we go, the more we see of the sacrifice of Jesus. But to begin with, the crowd cried 'Let him be crucified!' (Mt 27:22).

Pilate signalled that he wanted nothing to do with this man's death so he 'washed his hands' of the whole affair. Jesus was handed over to the soldiers where he was brought to receive his cross, the instrument of his death.

Dear Lord,

Help us not to be indifferent to the plight of innocent victims of suffering and violence. Give us the strength to stand up and be counted where there is injustice or untruth.

Amen.

Our Father ... Hail Mary ... Glory be ...
Have mercy on us, O Lord, have mercy on us.

THE SECOND STATION

Jesus Receives His Cross

We adore you, O Christ, and we bless you,
Because by your holy cross you have redeemed the world.

To mock Jesus, who was condemned as King of the Jews, the soldiers fashioned a crown made from thorns. It was roughly placed on the top of his head and the thorns cut into his forehead and skull quite deeply. Then, tied with ropes and bleeding from the savage and frenzied scourging, in an awful state, Jesus stumbled over to where the crosses were. There the soldiers laid a huge cross piece on his back and shoulders. The condemned man would carry his cross to Calvary, a hilly area just outside the city walls. Leading criminals through the streets to their place of execution was exactly what the Romans wanted to keep the level of fear up. Crucifixion was prominent and public and carried out for all to see, and it was an agonising act of public disgrace. The Romans did it primarily as a warning to everyone not to disturb the *Pax Romana*, the civic peace that they gifted to a country or region.

Soldiers led Jesus out along the narrow streets to the cheers and hisses of the bystanders who would have been both scared and excited at the same time. The condemned criminal would be jostled, tripped, and punched by the crowds and the soldiers would land blows and whips as they struggled and stumbled. Jesus would have heard swearing, cursing, screaming, mockery, and abuse as he felt the weight of the cross on his body. Some criminals would have given vulgarity and abuse back, but Jesus never made a sound and called out inwardly to the Father.

The journey to Calvary was short enough but to Jesus it would have been endless in terms of his exhaustion and pain as he had been up all night after the supper with his disciples. They had been heavy with sleep in the Garden of Gethsemane (Mt 26:40) and could barely keep their eyes open. Jesus was betrayed and arrested. All through the night and into the morning he was questioned and roughed up.

Lord,

So many people carry a cross. Many are in impossible situations; bereaved, ill, in broken relationships, condemned, worried, at the end of their tether. Every day we are aware of the struggles of families, of children, of the little ones. The pandemic has affected the entire world, millions have become sick and so many died. As you carried your cross, Jesus, you know our struggles. Give to all who suffer a sense of strength, peace, and healing.

Amen.

Our Father ... Hail Mary ... Glory be ...
Have mercy on us, O Lord, have mercy on us.

III.

THE THIRD STATION

Jesus Falls for the First Time

We adore you, O Christ, and we bless you,
Because by your holy cross you have redeemed the world.

Many parents put their young child against the wall and call on him or her to walk. From photos when I was young, to videos placed on social media today, friends and relatives can see the child take their first steps. Part of learning to walk is to stumble and fall. Mammy or Daddy catches the little one and puts them back against the wall for one more try. We all had to do it.

As we grow up, we are learning new things in the process. We are making mistakes and failing sometimes. The learner driver will be embarrassed as he or she stalls the engine and hops along the road. The trainee pilot will judge the progress of his or her instruction by how good their landing is. The student doctor will take seven years to complete basic training.

As a student friar, I took turns in the kitchen to cook for the community, and I collaborated with another student friar to see how he did it. Timing the meat, judging the softness of the spuds, one heaped spoonful of soup powder into the cold water, mix, and let it come to the boil. Until it came to measuring out the pasta for supper. In the community, I got my measurements right, and made a tasty sauce. So, I decided to make pasta for the family when I was home on holidays. Again, the sauce came out very well, but the problem was I made enough pasta for thirty people!

We all fall, and the trick is to get back up. Jesus falls for the first time, stumbling under the weight of the cross, but he climbs back up and keeps going. In Gethsemane Jesus says, 'My Father, if it is possible, let this cup pass from me; yet not what I want but what you want' (Mt 26:39).

Dear Lord,
Bless all who stumble and fall and fail in sin.
Teach us by the power of the Holy Spirit to get
back up and to begin again in faith and trust.
Amen.

Our Father ... Hail Mary ... Glory be ...
Have mercy on us, O Lord, have mercy on us.

THE FOURTH STATION

Jesus Meets His Beloved Mother

We adore you, O Christ, and we bless you,
Because by your holy cross you have redeemed the world.

This is one of the saddest scenes in the Stations of the Cross. The fourth station highlights the selflessness of parents: parents who in a heartbeat would switch places with their sick child; parents who stay in a hospital room as their child prepares for surgery; parents who go hungry to let their children eat when the food is scarce; parents who cross borders, deserts and seas to find safety, sanctuary and a new beginning for their families; parents who visit their child in prison when all others have given up on them; parents who see their child fail despite huge efforts; parents saying goodbye to their child as he or she starts school, leaves home or emigrates.

When I was a hospital chaplain, I witnessed a heartbroken mother lying in bed holding her dead son following the withdrawal of treatment, and I prayed with the mother when she and the family agreed to donate his organs to help another live and thrive. Mothers put their children first.

Mary always points to her son. In the Magnificat (Lk 1:46-55) she praises God first because he looked upon his lowly servant. At the wedding at Cana, she intercedes with Jesus to save the embarrassment of the groom and those in charge of the wedding. She advises them that they must 'do whatever he tells you' (Jn 2:1-11). Mary puts her son, Jesus, first.

I try to focus on the silent, painful love between Jesus and Mary. She dries his tears and without a word encourages him. Humanly speaking, it must have been heartbreaking for both. Then Jesus is pushed on, manhandled away from her to continue his Way of the Cross.

Lord, thou art hard on mothers:
We suffer in their coming and their going;
And tho' I grudge them not, I weary, weary
Of the long sorrow – And yet I have my joy:
My sons were faithful, and they fought.
('The Mother' by Pádraig Mac Piarais)

Our Father ... Hail Mary ... Glory be ...
Have mercy on us, O Lord, have mercy on us.

THE FIFTH STATION

Simon of Cyrene Helps Jesus to Carry the Cross

We adore you, O Christ, and we bless you,
Because by your holy cross you have redeemed the world.

Most people would have kept their heads down rather than attract the soldiers' attention. It was better not to come under their radar and therefore to keep out of their way. Roman soldiers were tough, well trained and ready to fight. Historians say there was one legion stationed in Jerusalem, as well as allies. A legion was around eight thousand soldiers in the Roman army. A centurion oversaw one hundred soldiers, and these soldiers were ruthless. They had orders to fiercely guard the *Pax Romana*, the Roman peace, which was a state of tranquillity kept across the Roman world in those years.

When Jesus was led out into the streets to be crucified, the soldiers beat and pushed him along the way, and they would also have been clearing the route ahead. Bystanders were eager to join in on the mockery as well as the hissing and spitting.

The soldiers noticed that Jesus was fast becoming unable to carry the cross and was beginning to fall under the weight. Sometimes the soldiers ordered people from the crowd to help, and they would accept no refusal. One did not refuse a directive from a well-armed, burly soldier equipped with whip, sword and spear.

They compelled a passer-by, Simon of Cyrene, to carry Jesus' cross (Mk 15:21-2). He was minding his own business and was suddenly made get involved. What could he do? While I am sure it crossed his mind that it was dangerous to help Jesus, who was in a pathetic state, Simon agreed to take the weight of the cross because he was afraid of what might happen if he tried to ignore or disobey the soldiers.

In the famous outdoor Stations of the Cross in San Giovanni Rotondo, the artist depicts Padre Pio as Simon of Cyrene. Here, Padre Pio willingly assists Jesus along the Way of the Cross and shares in his sufferings. All his life, Padre Pio carried the cross of Jesus in bearing the stigmata, and in suffering, until his death in 1968.

> Lord,
> We know that in the real world sometimes it can be dangerous to see things and to speak up, for fear that we can put ourselves or our families in danger. It can be safer to look the other way. Simon of Cyrene was someone who found himself suddenly involved in something he would have preferred to have nothing to do with. Help us through the intercession of Simon of Cyrene, who helped Jesus bear the cross, to find the right balance and always stay close to the truth.
> Amen.

Our Father ... Hail Mary ... Glory be ...
Have mercy on us, O Lord, have mercy on us.

THE SIXTH STATION

Veronica Wipes the Face of Jesus

We adore you, O Christ, and we bless you,
Because by your holy cross you have redeemed the world.

The condemned criminals ran the gauntlet of the mocking crowds who were whipped into a frenzy as they struggled out of the city towards the place of crucifixion. They were spat at, kicked, screamed at, pushed and jostled. On these terrible occasions, there was a lot of noise. Crucifixion was a public show put on by the Romans, designed to instil fear into the rabble. So, while there were people who mistreated the criminals passing by on the way to their awful deaths, there were also kind and charitable people and those who supported the criminals because they were on the same side. Veronica was a woman who was moved with sorrow for Jesus when she saw him as he passed. He cut a pathetic figure, bleeding and bruised with spittle and sweat covering him. She reached out with the clean cloth she was holding to wipe his face. Perhaps she did this every time there was a procession of criminals going that way. Maybe she lived close by, and this was something she liked to do. She may have thought it was a small thing, but the story is told to this day because of her encounter with Jesus.

Legend has it that his face was so disfigured after the abuse he suffered all night at the hands of the Pharisees and the Roman soldiers that its imprint was left on Veronica's cloth. She offered something simple, and it gave Jesus a moment of comfort and a chance to catch his breath. For a split second he felt human and there was someone along the way who did not swear, mock or curse him. And maybe Jesus became aware of the hundreds of criminals who met Veronica's non-judgemental charity and felt human.

Dear Lord,

Thank you for all who go out of their way, and go the extra mile, even in the face of opposition to help others, especially the most marginalised. Thank you Lord for these people who reach out despite the risk of opposition, or even when it may be unpopular.

Amen.

Our Father ... Hail Mary ... Glory be ...

Have mercy on us, O Lord, have mercy on us.

VII.

THE SEVENTH STATION
Jesus Falls for the Second Time

We adore you, O Christ, and we bless you,
Because by your holy cross you have redeemed the world.

Maybe this fall came immediately after Veronica tried to show Jesus some comfort and kindness. Once there was a pause in the progress of the criminals moving to the hill of Calvary, to get things moving again, the soldiers would have kicked out, lashed out and used more brutality. This moment of respite meant further pain and humiliation for Jesus, and perhaps when Jesus fell this time, he did not see it coming. In a split second, gravity takes over and Jesus is on the ground, pinned between the stones, the grit and the crossbeam on his shoulder blades. Waves of pain hurtle all around Jesus' body. Dizziness races across the top of his head, thanks to the crown of thorns the soldiers have made him wear in perverse mockery of the 'King of the Jews'.

He turns from Veronica and then falls like a building being demolished. For anyone watching the scene, it resembles the kid in school being knocked over by the bully to the ferocious laughter of all in the hallway. Here, however, there also might have been a hint of slow motion about this one for Jesus. He sees in a moment the blur of a fist, and *thud!* ... Then the sky, and *crack!* – the smell of the dust and stone mixed with blood and salty tears. His poor hands are trembling, and he is frightened again.

Dear Jesus,

Help us to support all our sisters and brothers when they fall. Give us patience with ourselves and others. God forgive those who knock others down, especially the little ones. God forgive us when we knock others down through carelessness, lack of awareness and short-sightedness.

Amen.

Our Father ... Hail Mary ... Glory be ...
Have mercy on us, O Lord, have mercy on us.

THE EIGHTH STATION

Jesus Meets the Women of Jerusalem

We adore you, O Christ, and we bless you,
Because by your holy cross you have redeemed the world.

As we have seen, the criminals have a terrible time making their way to the place of execution. They encounter many people along the way, varying from those who share in the mockery and the abuse to those who stare silently yet do not make eye contact. There are those who are genuinely upset for the condemned because they know how bad it will get judging by the previous crucifixions. Crucifixions were public, shameful and meant to attract great attention, as if to say 'do not let this happen to you'.

Jesus encounters some women who were gathered along the way, who were weeping and crying for the criminals, and perhaps for him too, as they would have known about him. The trial and condemnation of Jesus was being talked about around Jerusalem and they would have heard about the ferocious scourging he endured. Seeing him come along was a huge shock and when he got up close they could not help themselves, although some were not able to look at him, so disfigured did he look. Jesus managed to speak to them, and he counselled them not to weep for him but to weep for their children because he foresaw grim times ahead (Lk 23:28). He knew what hardships would befall these simple people and that life would not be easy going forward. Jesus was not just looking into the short-term future; he was also seeing much further down the road. The place where he walked that day would see pain and suffering for centuries to come.

Lord Jesus,

In the Gospel of St John, you prayed, 'May they all be one ...'. You asked the Father's help that your disciples would be united so that all will believe it was God who sent you. We pray too for those who live in your ancient homeland, troubled with violence and bloodshed. We offer hope that one day soon bridges of unity will be built there, rather than walls of division so that all, and especially the innocent ones, the little ones, will suffer no more.

Amen.

Our Father ... Hail Mary ... Glory be ...
Have mercy on us, O Lord, have mercy on us.

THE NINTH STATION

Jesus Falls for the Third Time

We adore you, O Christ, and we bless you,
Because by your holy cross you have redeemed the world.

Jesus is at the end of his tether. He is exhausted and can almost endure no more. He falls a third time. This is the hardest fall of all. Now the tank is empty, and the soldiers can see this.

For me, the ninth station represents all who just cannot go on and all who have had enough. It illustrates those who have been let down repeatedly and humiliated day after day. This station is for all who feel they have no way out and are scared and full of shame. There is no light out there and all is darkness. There is no lifeboat to clutch onto, the rough sea is enveloping the drowning soul and the Devil is mocking, using his old lies to shatter the broken spirit. It will take an almighty effort to climb back up.

The ninth station is for those who have hit rock bottom. It is for all who are in active addiction; all who battle alcohol, drugs, gambling, sexual addictions, etc., and deeply desire to change their lives against all the odds. This station is for all who have been beaten to the ground repeatedly.

A woman in recovery once told me her story and about how she slipped back into addiction along the way; 'Even Jesus fell three times ...'.

I remember being told of a man who said, 'It was only when I hit rock bottom that I hit the Rock of Ages.'

Another man, in recovery one day at a time after many years of drinking, said, 'There's only one thing worse than being lost – it's when nobody is looking for you.'

This ninth station is for all who feel they have failed.

Jesus got up.

We can all get up with God's help and the help of one another. With the help of the Higher Power. A day at a time.

Lord Jesus,

Help us to get up when we fall. Help us to help each other along the way. Teach us that no one is a 'write-off' – that all are made in God's image and likeness.

Amen.

Our Father ... Hail Mary ... Glory be ...
Have mercy on us, O Lord, have mercy on us.

THE TENTH STATION

Jesus is Stripped of His Garments

We adore you, O Christ, and we bless you,
Because by your holy cross you have redeemed the world.

The criminals come to the Place of the Skull and the soldiers prepare to crucify the three men condemned that day. The crosses are erected overlooking the city and people are gathered nearby because the soldiers have cordoned off the immediate area.

They begin to strip the clothes from the condemned men. They roughly tear the outer garments and under garments from them. Again, crucifixion is meant to humiliate and make a mockery of the criminal. There is no dignity for the condemned here.

When the clothes are torn from Jesus, the vicious wounds from the scourging are exposed and the ferocity of the soldiers manhandling him maximises the pain. He looks terrible and even the hardest hearts avert their eyes at the terrible sight. They throw his clothes and his robe aside and will cast lots for it in an hour or so while they wait for him to die.

In the tenth station, I see all whose dignity has been robbed. The way people have been humiliated in public for all the world to see. The tenth station can represent a prayer for all who have had their bodies, their person and their dignity exploited and degraded sexually. The multi-billion-dollar pornography industry dehumanises everyone, all who have used it and those who have been used by it. The glamorisation of violence too is another shocking illustration of how human dignity and the human person are increasingly abused.

The tenth station is a prayer for all who have been mocked in public because they have stepped up and because their standards and values are not what society wants to hear, they are torn down, trolled and bullied on social media platforms.

Dear Lord,

Help us to see that all human life is sacred, from the moment of conception to the moment of natural death. Forgive me for falling short at times in the high calling you give to all people in the way I may have treated others.

Amen.

Our Father ... Hail Mary ... Glory be ...
Have mercy on us, O Lord, have mercy on us.

THE ELEVENTH STATION
Jesus is Nailed to the Cross

We adore you, O Christ, and we bless you,
Because by your holy cross you have redeemed the world.

The brutality of the Roman soldiers would have come to a head now as they began to take out the implements of crucifixion. Forget about the clean, polished and technologically advanced tools found in the hardware superstore: hammers, nails, screwdrivers and lengths of timber for the use in the home or trade. The tools the Romans used were vulgar, cumbersome and designed to be painful. The nails they used to fasten hands and feet to the cross were large and more akin to the bolts and brackets one would see fixing shelves to a wall today. To get some idea of the kind of treatment Jesus endured just look again at Mel Gibson's *The Passion of the Christ* starring Jim Caviezel.

The Roman soldiers roughly stretched the arms of Jesus between the two ends of the cross beam and began to hammer the bolts into the hands and then the feet. The pain would have been excruciating. He could not catch his breath for the trauma his body felt. When his body was fixed to the cross complete with ropes to hold his arms to the wooden cross beam, they raised the cross to a standing position. In order to breathe, Jesus would have to lift himself up, causing yet another electric jolt of pain through his feet and hands.

Padre Pio was known to have a shoulder wound, which he admitted to one of the friars caused him great pain. This seems to correspond to the damage from the cross beam as Jesus carried the cross, and as he hung there and tried to take a breath. As Jesus struggled to look around, through horrific pain, he could gasp a prayer asking the Father to forgive those who condemned and crucified him (Lk 23:34).

There was a lot of activity as the soldiers finished crucifying Jesus and the two criminals, and some people in the crowd drew closer to the crosses. The soldiers, armed with spears and whips, kept an eye on everyone in case of any disturbance.

Most people kept their distance to wait for the men to die. Others began to head home, the 'show' over. Still others waited as there was talk of a miracle. Some were calling for Jesus to come down from the cross.

> Lord,
> You call on us to always be prepared to forgive:
> 'seventy-seven times' (Mt 18:22). Help us to learn
> to forgive others and to ask for forgiveness from
> those we have hurt.
> Amen.

Our Father ... Hail Mary ... Glory be ...
Have mercy on us, O Lord, have mercy on us.

THE TWELFTH STATION

Jesus Dies on the Cross

We adore you, O Christ, and we bless you,
Because by your holy cross you have redeemed the world.

Romans crucified criminals in public to teach a severe lesson to the one on the cross just as much as those who were witnessing the grotesque scene. Often for days after the event, the bodies would be left hanging to decompose or be attacked by stray animals, again as a warning to the people. It did not matter to the Romans; the ones crucified were seen as non-persons, the scum of the earth. Their bodies, their memories held no value and were consigned to the dump of humanity.

The drama of the slow death of Jesus was played out from the morning until the afternoon so he died in agony, slowly suffocating and eventually bleeding to death. It was surely a horrific thing for those who loved him to witness – not least his mother, Mary. Her mind racing, she must have remembered through the panic, the trauma and the tears, the prophecy of old Simeon when she and Joseph presented the baby Jesus in the temple all those years before: 'This child is destined for the falling and the rising of many in Israel, and to be a sign that will be opposed ... and a sword will pierce your own soul too' (Lk 2:34-5).

Humanly speaking, Jesus must have struggled with so much as he choked and cried out. Through the electrifying tinnitus, the clamour of mockery and madness persisted. Jesus is true God and true man, and he did not cling to his equality with God but emptied himself, taking on the form of a slave (Phil 2:6-11). For her part, Mary the mother of Jesus kept the faith because deep down she knew who her son was. The Angel Gabriel told Mary that he would be called 'Son of the Most High' (Lk 1:32). I imagine at home in Nazareth and in her later encounters with Jesus, particularly as he travelled around, Mary probably related to him as human and may therefore have felt fearful as she saw some of the negative reactions to his words and powerful deeds.

Only a mother who has witnessed the suffering and death of her child will understand what Mary went through as she stood at the foot of the cross. We need to park the saccharine view of Mary and Joseph as merely 'plaster statues' or 'paintings' and therefore beyond our reach. They lived in a tough world and now from heaven they are more than qualified to understand our struggles and pray to God for us. They are holy in truth because they suffered yet they kept the faith. They said yes to God.

Jesus' conversation with the thief on the cross shows how, right up to the point of death, in agony and excruciating pain, he is prepared to forgive and guide sinful and broken humanity right into the kingdom of heaven. He asks no questions and responds in mercy to the open heart of the one crucified alongside him (Lk 23:43). We can be confident that he has a place for us as we call out, 'Jesus, remember me when you come into your kingdom' (Lk 23:42). On the Sunday after he was elected, Pope Francis preached in the church of St Anna in the Vatican. In his homily the pope said, 'The message of Jesus is mercy. For me, and I say this with humility, it is the Lord's strongest message.'

After hours of a slow and agonising death, Jesus gives up his spirit. The time comes for the soldiers to finish and so they begin to kill off the criminals. They break the legs of the two criminals on either side of Jesus and then the soldier drives a sword into Jesus' side to finish him off, but he is already dead.

A darkness began to fall over the land and people felt a strange chill as if a light had gone out. Those who gathered at the foot of the cross, including Mary, the mother of Jesus, and John, the beloved disciple, were heartbroken. Their spirits died on Calvary too on the eve of the Passover. They were totally lost and did not know what to do. 'It is finished'(Jn 19:30).

He was despised and rejected by others;
a man of suffering and acquainted with infirmity;
and as one from whom others hide their faces
he was despised, and we held him of no account.
Surely, he has borne our infirmities
and carried our diseases;
yet we accounted him stricken,
struck down by God, and afflicted.
But he was wounded for our transgressions,
crushed for our iniquities;
upon him was the punishment that made us
    whole,
and by his bruises we are healed.

(Is 53:3-5)

Our Father .... Hail Mary ... Glory be ...
Have mercy on us, O Lord, have mercy on us.

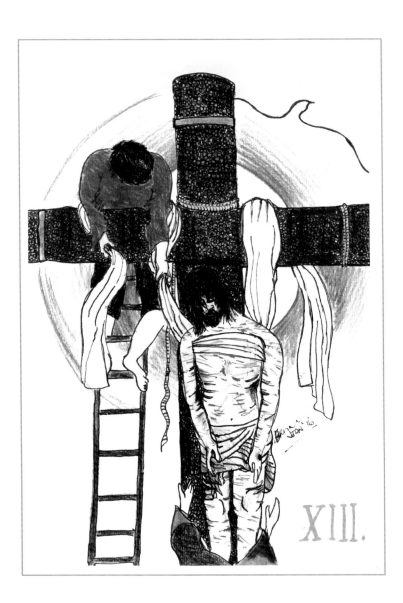

Jesus is Taken Down from the Cross

We adore you, O Christ, and we bless you,
Because by your holy cross you have redeemed the world.

There was a rush to take the bodies down from the cross this time. Usually, after a crucifixion they were left hanging there day and night as a warning to anyone who would dare to mess with the Romans. As the Passover was being celebrated from sundown,

Pilate made the decision to allow the bodies to be taken down. Pilate seems to cave into the Pharisees and Scribes who have huge power and control over the population. Despite having no power to exercise force except for the Temple Guard, the established church leadership tried to rule over the hearts and minds of people with a whole plethora of laws. The Romans were not as influential over the people in the way the church leadership were, but the people had no choice against such military might that they preferred to save their necks than face severe violence.

The body of Jesus was lowered down and laid at the feet of those who followed him. There is that poignant scene of Mary holding his dead body as she wept bitterly. She held him from the moment of his conception; she held him as a tiny baby, as a little boy, and in her heart when he became a man. Now she holds his lifeless body, having become the mother of all humanity according to one final act of Jesus (Jn 19:25-9).

Lovely Lady dressed in blue, teach me how to
  pray!
God was just your little boy, tell me what to say.
Did you lift him up sometimes, gently on your
  knee?
Did you sing to him the way mother does to me?
Did you hold his hand at night? And did you
  ever try
Telling him stories of the world? O! And did he
  cry?
Do you really think he cares if I tell him things?
Little things that happen? And do the Angels'
  wings make a noise?
Can he hear me if I speak low? Does he
  understand me now?
Tell me for you know.
Lovely lady dressed in blue, teach me how to pray
God was just your little boy, and you know the
  way.

('Lovely Lady Dressed in Blue'
by Mary Dixon Thayer)

Our Father ... Hail Mary ... Glory be ...
Have mercy on us, O Lord, have mercy on us.

THE FOURTEENTH STATION

Jesus' Body is Placed in the Tomb

We adore you, O Christ, and we bless you,
Because by your holy cross you have redeemed the world.

As it was the evening before the Passover, the followers of Jesus, including some women who were his disciples, had to hurry to place the body of Jesus in a borrowed tomb. They hardly had time to anoint the body with herbs, spices and oils, and no time to properly dress the body with a clean shroud. They would have to wait until the morning of the third day to spend more time anointing the body of Jesus. In the meantime, they had to arrange men to place the heavy stone across the entrance to seal it.

There had been rumours that some of Jesus' followers would be in danger of stealing the body and starting a rumour that he had risen. Again, to placate the Pharisees and the Scribes who were not satisfied that Jesus was dead, Pilate arranged to have soldiers stand guard at the entrance to the tomb to make sure no followers of Jesus would take the body from the tomb. And so, for the first and second night there was no chance anyone would get away with stealing the body of Jesus, as with the soldiers standing guard it would be too dangerous to mess with them. And neither was there any danger that a Roman soldier would fall asleep on the job. This simply did not happen.

Dear Lord,

We pray for all who have died and gone before us marked with the sign of faith. We remember the souls of the faithful departed and commend them all to your mercy as we are reminded by our Holy Father, Pope Francis that 'mercy is the beating heart of the Gospel'.

Amen.

Our Father ... Hail Mary ... Glory be ...
Have mercy on us, O Lord, have mercy on us.

THE FIFTEENTH STATION

The Resurrection from the Dead

We adore you, O Christ, and we bless you,
Because by your holy cross you have redeemed the world.

I am not sure when the fifteenth station was added to the traditional Stations of the Cross. I have seen some churches where there is a fifteenth station of the cross. However, as far as I am aware most churches still have only fourteen around their walls. The addition of the fifteenth station is a powerful reminder that when the body of Jesus was hastily laid in the tomb, that was not the end. The body of Jesus lay there until that first Easter Sunday morning when Jesus rose from the dead. Fundamentally, this is a call to faith. Jesus rose from the dead because he said he would: 'Then he began to teach them that the Son of Man must undergo great suffering, and be rejected by the elders, the chief priests, and the scribes, and be killed, and after three days rise again' (Mk 8:31).

The first encounters with the risen Lord were with the women who hurried to the tomb hoping to find someone to roll away the huge stone and then set about the task of properly anointing the body of Jesus. However, they arrived early on the morning of the third day only to find the stone had been rolled back, and men in brilliant white urged them not to look among the dead for one who lives (Lk 24:1-5). Mary of Magdala encountered the Lord himself but was prevented from recognising him at first (Jn 20:11-14). Later that day, two of his disciples were walking away from Jerusalem on the road to Emmaus when Jesus came up and walked with them. Jesus himself helps them to recognise the risen Lord in the scriptures and at the breaking of the bread (Lk 24:13-35). They could not contain their joyful enthusiasm when they realised it was Jesus, so much so that they had to return to Jerusalem and to the other disciples to tell them of what had happened on the road.

This is the result of any encounter with the risen Lord. Jesus touches people, primarily on the inside, where they are then moved to action. The task is to flee from the night-time of doubt into the bright light of faith. The believing Christian has no business in the darkness of the empty tomb: we must come out into the daylight. Early on Sunday morning, Jesus bursts out of the tomb, the firstborn from the dead. Fifty days later he sends the Holy Spirit, the Sanctifier, to empower the apostles and Mary, the early church. The apostles and the other followers of Jesus were strengthened to go about the world preaching the good news and baptising people in the name of the Father, and of the Son, and of the Holy Spirit (Mt 28:16-20). Today, we are witnesses to this.

> Risen Jesus,
> As we have walked the Way of the Cross with you, lead us from darkness into light. Help us not just to be good Christians but holy people by the grace of your Holy Spirit. Sanctify your church with the help of the prayers of Mary, your mother.
> Amen.

Our Father ... Hail Mary ... Glory be ...
Have mercy on us, O Lord, have mercy on us.

CONCLUDING PRAYER

Almighty, eternal, just and merciful God
Grant us in our misery the grace to do
For your sake alone what we know you want us to do
And always to desire what pleases you.
Thus inwardly cleansed,
Interiorly enlightened
And enflamed by the fire of the Holy Spirit
We may be able to follow in the footprints
Of your beloved Son, Our Lord Jesus,
And so make our way to you, Most High,
By your grace alone
Who live and reign
In perfect Trinity and in simple unity
One all-powerful God
For ever and ever. Amen.

(Prayer at the end of 'A Letter to the
Entire Order' by St Francis of Assisi)